AF271840

Adventures WITH BODIE THE English Bulldog

IN WISCONSIN

BY TNK

"My name is Bodie, the traveling English Bulldog. Come be my friend and join me on my travels to all 50 states."

Printed in the United States of America
First Printing, 2019
ISBN: 978-1-54398-680-8

My name is Bodie and I am an English Bulldog. I am
5 years old and my birthday is on January 28, 2014.

My life is a little different than most dogs because I travel in an RV with my mom and dad. I am on a mission to visit all 50 states in the United States of America. My RV is just like your home, but it's on wheels and gets pulled behind our truck when we travel to a new state.

My life started in Wisconsin. I lived in a small town in the western part of the state for the first year of my life. This was before I got to live in an RV, but it was still a lot of fun!

Summer in Wisconsin is sunny and warm. Sometimes the temperature can get up to almost 100 degrees!

Bulldogs can have a hard time breathing when
it's hot outside, so my mom got me a pool
to hang out in when it got REALLY hot.

Every once in a while, we got to go to grandma & grandpa's house. They lived on a lake, which was WAY bigger than my pool. Did you know that Wisconsin has over 15,000 lakes?

One time my mom took me out on the kayak with her. She made me wear my life jacket to stay safe, just in case I fell in.

It was probably a good thing she did because.... guess what!!! I FELL IN!

And oh man, was that a shock. I had no idea what to do.

Just then, mom pulled me back up on the kayak. I made sure I stayed on the inside for the rest of our ride.

Wisconsin is known as the Dairy State. That means there are lots of cows, lots of ice cream, and lots of cheese. The ice cream sundae was even invented in Wisconsin.

My mom says that chocolate is not good for bulldogs, so my favorite ice cream sundae has strawberries and bananas on it.

Fall is probably my favorite time of year in Wisconsin. It's not too hot, but not too cold. All of the leaves turn from green to all sorts of colors, like red, orange, and yellow.

We get to have campfires, go on long walks in the forest, and play in the creeks. Did you know almost half of the land in Wisconsin is covered by forest?!

When the leaves fall off the trees, they get really crunchy. This is a bummer, because it makes it hard to sneak up on squirrels and bunnies.

Beside the perfect temperatures and pretty colors, fall also marks the start of football season. My favorite football team is the Green Bay Packers (my mom told me so).

When it's game day and football is on TV, I always follow mom around really close because she usually has snacks!

Oh boy, do I love snacks. I just have to be careful how much I eat so I can stay healthy.

In the winter, Wisconsin gets very cold. It is actually considered one of the coldest places in the United States. Sometimes the temperatures are below zero. Can you believe that?

I don't have long hair like some of my friends, so I have to make sure I wear my hat and mittens.

The first time I saw snow, I got really excited.
It looked so soft and fluffy! Wisconsin gets
on average 5 feet of snow every year.

I rushed outside and did a couple laps of zoomies! Zoomies are what I call it when I get really hyper and run around really fast and crazy.

I did not realize how cold the snow really was until after I was done with my zoomies. All four of my little paws were just frozen!

After my feet warmed up and I took a nap, I found mom and dad. I told them I wanted to move to Colorado and play in the snow in the mountains all the time.

Mom and dad said we could
and I was so excited!

I hope you will be my friend and come read
with me about my life in Colorado.

Colorado! Here I come!

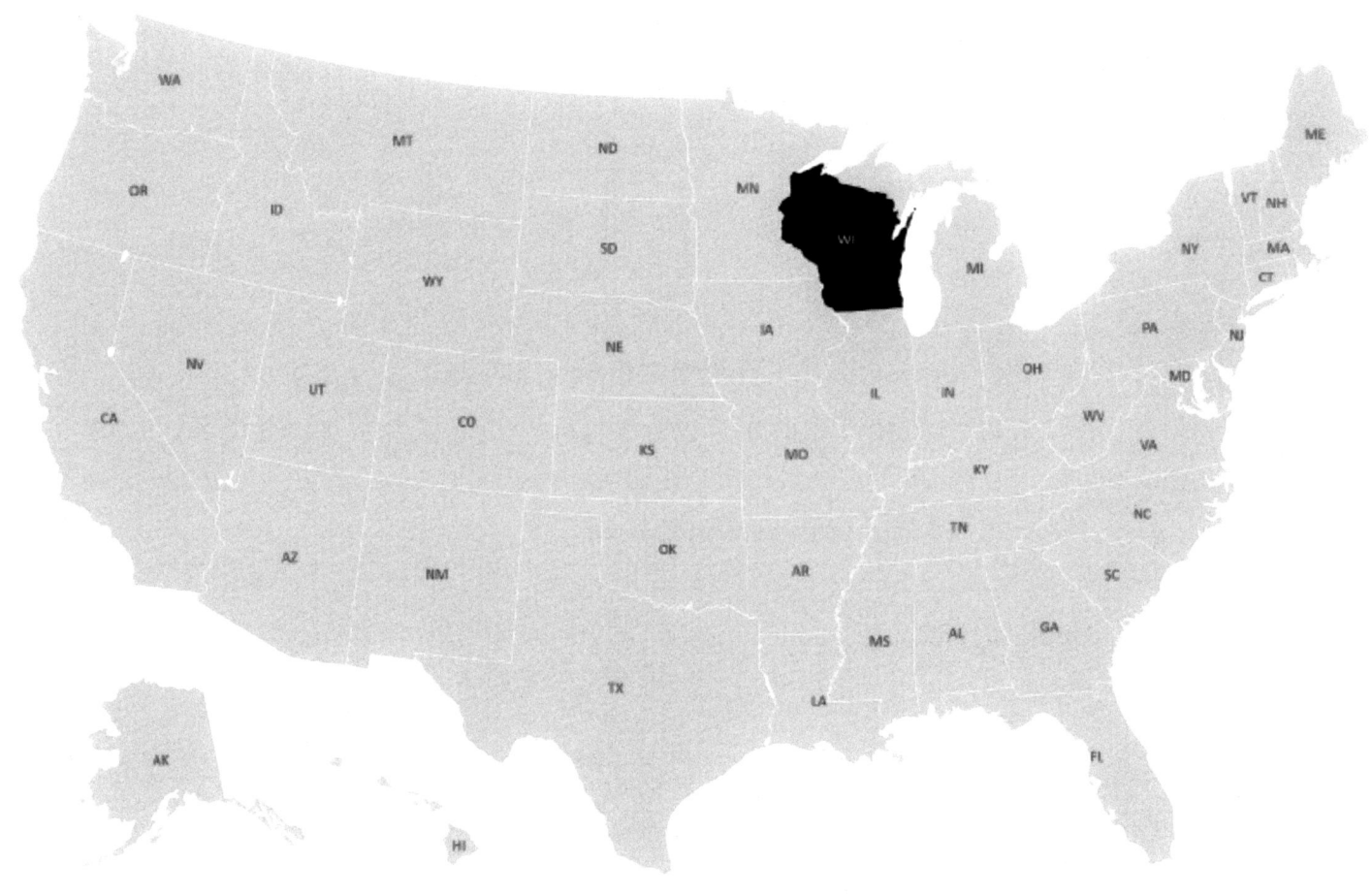

This is a map of the United States of America and the highlighted state above is Wisconsin. This is where I am at! Where are you?

Follow me and read about my adventures to every state!

Author's Note

Hi Everyone, Trevor & Katie ("TnK") here! Adventures with Bodie the English Bulldog is based on true stories and adventures we have had in our life. We are currently living fulltime in an RV traveling the US. We decided that our stories & all the laughs we've had while traveling with Bodie were things everyone should be able to enjoy. The photos you see on each page are actual photos from the state in which the book is based on. We are planning to write a educational children's storybook for each state that we visit. It is our hope that we can provide family fun and a few laughs while you follow along with our journey through the eyes of Bodie the English Bulldog.

Follow our journey below!
Instagram: @bodietheenglishbulldog
Website/Blog: www.bodietheenglishbulldog.com